DECEMBER
MONTHLY
ACTIVITIES

Written by Mary Ellen Sterling and Susan Schumann Nowlin

Illustrated by: Blanqui Apodaca, Paula Spence, Keith Vasconcelles and Theresa Wright

Teacher Created Materials, Inc.
P.O. Box 1040
Huntington Beach, CA 92647
©1989 Teacher Created Materials, Inc.
Made in U.S.A.

ISBN 1-55734-154-0

The classroom teacher may reproduce copies of materials in this book for classroom use only. The reproduction of any part for an entire school or school system is strictly prohibited. No part of this publication may be transmitted, stored, or recorded in any form without written permission from the publisher.

Table of Contents

Table of Contents

Introduction

December Monthly Activities provides 80 dynamic pages of ready-to-use resources, ideas and activities that students love! All are centered around the themes, special dates and holidays of the month.

A complete "month-in-a-book," it includes:

- *A Calendar of Events* - ready to teach from and filled with fascinating information about monthly events, PLUS lots of fun ways you can apply these useful facts in your classroom.

- *A Whole Language Integrated Teaching Unit* - theme-based planning strategies, projects, lessons, activities, and more that provide a practical, yet imaginative approach to a favorite seasonal topic.

- *People, Places and Events* - an exciting series of activities that relate to the daily events in the Calendar of Events, and provide an innovative way for students to reinforce skills.

- *Management Pages* - a supply of reproducible pages that take you through the month, providing a wealth of valuable organizational aids that are right at your fingertips.

- *A Bulletin Board* - featuring a "hands-on" approach to learning; complete with full-size patterns, step-by-step directions, and tips for additional ways you can use the board.

Ideas and activities are also included for:

- *math*
- *art projects*
- *reading*
- *science*

- *geography*
- *social studies*
- *stationery*
- *creative writing*

- *literature ideas*
- *cooking*
- *reports*
- *seasonal words*

December Monthly Activities is the most complete seasonal book you'll ever find, and its convenient, reproducible pages will turn each month into a special teaching—and learning—experience!

Using The Pages

December Monthly Activities brings you a wealth of easy-to-use, fun-filled activities and ideas that will help you make the most of December's special themes and events. Although most of the activities are designed to be used within this month, if the holidays and traditions vary in your location, you may easily adapt the pages to fit your needs. Here are some tips for getting the most from your pages:

CALENDAR OF EVENTS

Each day makes note of a different holiday, tells about a famous person or presents a historical event. A question relating to each topic is provided (answers are on page 76). Teachers can use these facts in any number of ways including:

- *Post a copy of the calendar on a special bulletin board. Each day assign a different student to find the answer to that day's question. Set aside some time during the day to discuss the question with the whole class.*

- *Write the daily fact on the chalkboard. Have students keep a handwriting journal and copy the fact first thing each morning. They must use their best handwriting, of course!*

- *Use a daily event, holiday or famous person as a springboard for a Whole Language theme. Brainstorm with the class to find out what they already know about the topic. Explore the topic through literature, the arts, language and music.*

- *Older students can write a report on any of the daily topics. Younger students can be directed to draw a picture of the historical event or figure.*

- *Have students make up their own questions to go along with the day's event!*

- *Assign each student a different day of the calendar. Have them present a short oral report to the class on that day's topic.*

- *Use the daily events for math reinforcement. Ask how many: Days, weeks, months and years since the event occurred (for a real brain teaser, have students compute hours, minutes and seconds).*

- *Use in conjunction with the People, Places and Events section (pages 32 - 46).*

BLANK CALENDAR

Copy a calendar for each student. Have students use them to:

- *Write in daily assignments; check off each one as completed.*

- *Set daily goals—behavioral or academic.*

- *Copy homework assignments.*

- *Fill in with special dates, holidays, classroom or school events.*

- *Keep track of classroom chores.*

- *Use as a daily journal of feelings.*

- *Make ongoing lists of words to learn to spell.*

- *Answer the Question of the Day (see Calendar of Events).*

- *Record daily awards (stamps, stickers, etc.) for behavior or academic achievement.*

- *At the end of the day, evaluate their attitude, behavior, class work, etc. and give them a grade and explanation for the grade.*

- *Log reading time and number of pages read for free reading time.*

- *If there are learning centers in the classroom, let students keep track of work they have completed at each one or copy a schedule of times and days they may use the centers.*

- *Each day, write at least one new thing they learned.*

MANAGEMENT PAGES

Nifty ideas for extending the use of these pages.

- **Contracts** — *Help students set long or short term goals such as keeping a clean desk, reading extra books or improving behavior.*

- **Awards** — *Show students you appreciate them by giving awards for good attitude, helping, being considerate or for scholastic achievement. Students can give them to each other, their teacher or the principal!*

- **Invitations** — *Invite parents, grandparents, friends or another class to a classroom, school or sports event.*

- **Field Trip** — *Use for class trips or have students use in planning their own field trip to another country or planet.*

- **Supplies** — *Tell parents when you need art, craft, classroom, physical education or any other kind of supplies.*

- **Record Form** — *Place names in alphabetical order to keep track of classroom chores, completed assignments, contracts or permission slips.*

- **Stationery** — *Use as a creative writing pattern, for correspondence with parents, or for homework assignments.*

- **News** — *Fill in with upcoming weekly events and send home on Monday or let students fill in each day and take home on Friday. Younger students may draw a picture of something special they did or learned.*

- **Clip Art** — *Decorate worksheets, make your own stationery or answer pages. Enlarge and use for bulletin boards.*

Hot Tips!

Be sure to look for the hot tips at the beginning of each section—they provide quick, easy and fun ways of extending the activities!

© *Teacher Created Materials, Inc. 1989*

December Highlights

- Calendar of Events
- Spelling Activities
- Story Starters
- Gameboard
- Poetry
- Art Project
- And More!

Hot Tips!

December is a festive month filled with special celebrations. Explore the traditions that are observed in other countries: St. Nicholas Day, Poinsettia Day, Feast of Santa Lucia, Christmas, Boxing Day, Hanukkah, and New Year's. It's a perfect way to introduce other countries and their customs.

DECEMBER

December is the last month of the year. Its name comes from the Latin word decem which means ten. In the Roman calendar, December was the tenth month.

Flower - Narcissus: Birthday - Turquoise:

1

What birthdays or anniversaries does your family celebrate this month?

St. Nicholas Day (Great Britain)

6

Who is St. Nicholas?

Madame Tussaud was born on this day in 1761 in London.

7

What is found in her famous museum?

American inventor Eli Whitney was born on this day in 1765.

8

Although he is most famous for his cotton gin, he also developed this procedure. What is it?

Poinsettia Day Dr. Poinsett introduced this plant to the U.S.

12

Where did this plant originate?

Feast of Santa Lucia, the patron saint of light.

13

Which countries celebrate this day?

The South Pole was discovered on this day in 1911.

14

In which continent is the South Pole located?

The word December comes from the Latin word for ten.

19

What other words are based on "ten" ?

Anniversary of the Louisiana Purchase in 1803.

20

From which country did the U.S. buy this territory?

The first crossword puzzle in an American newspaper appeared in the *New York Sunday World* in 1913.

21

What is an anagram?

James Oglethorpe, founder of Georgia, born in 1696.

22

Why was Georgia called a "debtor's colony?"

Boxing Day (first week day after Christmas) Special boxed gifts are given to household and public servants.

26

Who is someone you don't often thank but would like to?

Louis Pasteur born in 1882.

27

What purification process bears his name?

Chewing gum was first patented in 1869 by William Semple.

28

What is your favorite brand of chewing gum?

Texas was admitted to the Union in 1845.

29

What is the state nickname of Texas?

French artist George Seurat was born in 1859. **2** *What is pointillism?*	Gilbert Stuart, famous portrait artist, was born on this day in 1755. **3** *What is a portrait?*	Day of the Artisans In Mexico, a day to honor laborers. **4** *On which day does the U.S. honor laborers?*	Birthdate of motion-picture producer Walt Disney in 1901. **5** *Where is the EPCOT Center located?*
	Clarence Birdseye, inventor of a new way to freeze food, was born in 1886. **9** *What kind of frozen foods do you eat?*	Mississippi admitted to the Union in 1817. **10** *What is the capital of Mississippi?*	UNICEF was created in 1946. **11** *What is an acronym?*
Birthdate of French engineer Alexandre Gustav Eiffel. **15** *How tall is the Eiffel Tower?*	Ludwig Van Beethoven, musical composer, born in 1770. **16** *Which of his senses did Beethoven lose before his 30th birthday?*	In 1903, Wilbur and Orville Wright made the first powered airplane flight. **17** *How long did the flight last?*	The 13th amendment was ratified in 1865. **18** *What did this amendment abolish?*
Only eight more days left until the New Year! **23** *How many hours is that? How many minutes?*	"Silent Night" was composed in 1818 on Christmas Eve. **24** *Who wrote the music for "Silent Night"?*	Christmas **25** *What customs or traditions does your family observe?*	
English writer Rudyard Kipling born in 1865. **30** *What is* **The Jungle Book** *about?*	New Year's Eve **31** *What are some New Year's resolutions you will make?*		Other holidays celebrated this month: ■ *Hanukkah the Jewish "Festival of Lights"* ■ *Kwanzaa, a seven-day African heritage celebration* ■ *December 21 is the first day of winter*

December

SUNDAY	MONDAY	TUESDAY	WEDNESDAY	THURSDAY	FRIDAY	SATURDAY

© *Teacher Created Materials, Inc. 1989*

December Words and Activities

December Word Bank

decorations	carols	December	green
elf	wreath	ivy	winter
reindeer	star	red	Christmas
mittens	presents	menorah	chimney
ornaments	merry	tree	ice skate
angel	dreidel	mistletoe	Rudolph
poinsettia	Noël	white	eve
snow	holly	wonderland	sleigh
bells	candy cane	stocking	gingerbread
Santa Claus	Hanukkah	candles	ski

Spelling Activities

Give the students a choice of assignments below or have them try one of the following ideas in place of the standard spelling lesson.

- *Draw stars or bells or stockings. Write a word from the Word Bank on each picture.*

- *Write eight words using cake frosting. Write the words on a gingerbread shape (see page 26 for pattern).*

- *Use pieces of red or green ribbon to write five words; glue to tagboard.*

- *Illustrate six words. Next to each, make a space for each letter. Have a friend do your worksheet.* ___ ___ ___ ___

- *Cut strips of construction paper. Write one word on each strip. Make a chain with the strips.*

Story Starters

☐ December is traditionally a time for gift-giving and remembering our loved ones. Have students write about their family's gift-giving experiences, or let them choose from one of the titles below.

- *The Best Gift I Ever Made*
- *The Year I Thought Santa Forgot Me*
- *How I Saved Christmas*
- *The Best Hanukkah Ever*
- *A Special Gift for My _____*

☐ Group students in teams of four or five. Give each group a large sheet of construction paper (12" x 18") and have them fold it into thirds. In the first section write the heading NOUNS; in the middle third write the heading ADJECTIVES; in the last section write VERBS. (Younger students could use headings such as THINGS, DESCRIBING WORDS, and ACTION WORDS.) Set a kitchen timer for ten minutes and have each group brainstorm Winter Words for each category. Then each member of the group chooses one word from each category and writes a sentence using all three words. Finally, as a group, they use all the sentences in one cooperative effort. Set aside some time for groups to share their creative stories.

☐ Writing alphabetical sentences can be a real challenge and fun for everyone. Brainstorm with the class and write words that are related to winter or to a special December holiday; this will give students a handy reference to use. Pairs or small groups can work on this project. Assign a sequence of letters to each pair or group. For example, abcde, or nopq, etc. Each pair or group must write a sentence in which the words begin with those letters in that order.

A *b*ig *c*loud's *d*rops *e*vaporated.
*N*oel *o*pened *p*resents *q*uickly.

Name _____ Date _____

Holiday Graph

Draw each holiday symbol on the proper point of the graph below. Coordinates are listed next to each symbol.

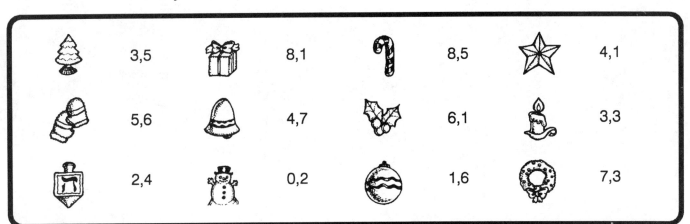

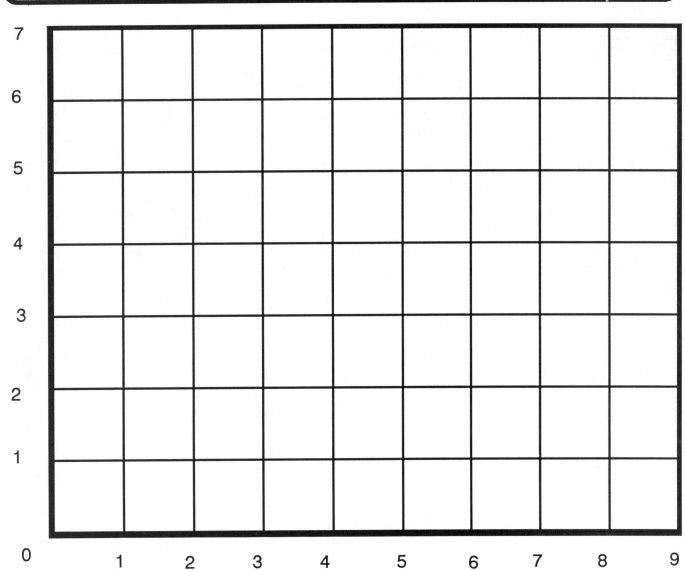

Name _____ **Skill** _____

December Worksheet

Directions: _____

_____

1.

2.

3.

4.

5.

6.

7.

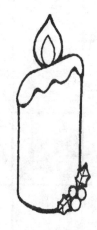
8.

Answers:

Santa's Sack

All the vowels are missing in the words below! Use the letters in Santa's sack to fill in the blanks.

1. c __ ndyc __ n __

2. g __ ng __ rbr __ __ d

3. r __ __ nd __ __ r

4. sn __ wfl __ k __

5. wr __ __ th

6. __ lf

7. h __ lly

8. g __ fts

9. c __ r __ ls

10. st __ r

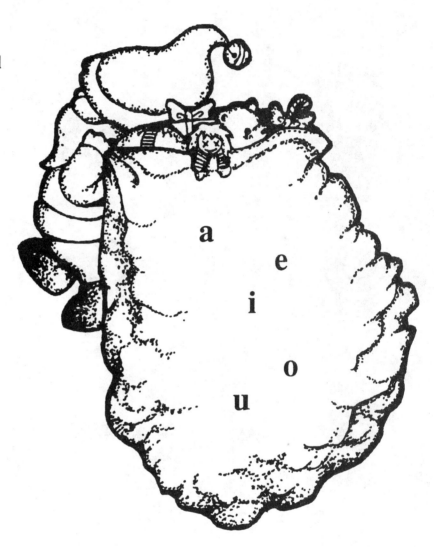

WORD BANK

elf	snowflake	holly	star
reindeer	gingerbread	candy cane	carols
	wreath	gifts	

Sugarland Gameboard

Use this generic gameboard for any subject area. Label each treat with a different math fact or science term or prefix, etc. (For more ideas see pages 79 and 80.) Each player will need a marker. Players can move one space at a time or determine the number of spaces moved with a die.

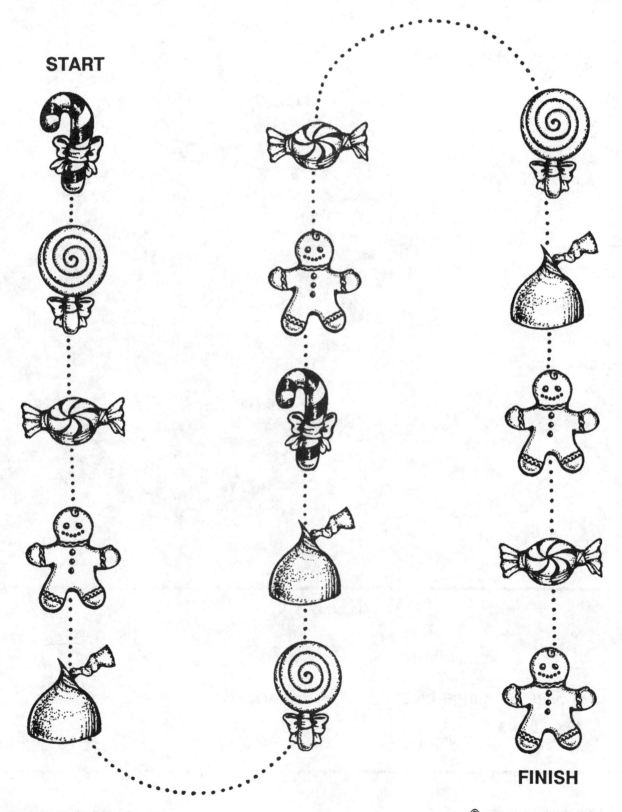

START

FINISH

16

© Teacher Created Materials, Inc. 1989

Game Page

Pass It On - An Indoor Game

You may have students remain seated if their desks are in rows or you may rearrange the furniture temporarily so that students can stand in columns. Form teams with equal numbers in each. Give a ball (a beach ball works well, but a rubber ball will do) to the first person in each column. At the signal, the ball is passed backward over the head until it reaches the last person in the column. Once the ball reaches the last person, he goes to the front of the column as everyone moves back one space. Continue the relay until all players are back in their original places.

Explosion - An Outdoor Game

The teacher stands in the middle of a large, unobstructed outdoor area and the students gather around the teacher. The following procedure should be explained to the students before play begins. At a given signal the students "explode" and run as far from the teacher as possible until the teacher blows the whistle. When students hear the whistle, they must hop backwards and return to the center to surround the teacher. Play continues in this manner, but each explosion can be followed by a different movement such as skipping, hopping on one foot, taking long strides, etc.

Poetry Page

■ **Name Poems**

With the class, brainstorm a list of words that describes their classmates. Use this list as an easy reference for this writing activity. On a sheet of paper, have students write their name down in a column. Pick some words from the list and write them across from the letters. Each descriptive word should begin with the same letter that begins that row (see example below).

■ **Rhyme That Name**

A variation of the Name Poem, above, is this version: Rhyme That Name. First choose a name (fictitious or real). Then make a list of words that rhyme with the last name. For the first line, write the name. The second line should be a rhyming sentence about the person. For example,

Tommy Moon   Debra Free

Was born in June.   Can climb a tree.

■ **Christmas Re-write**

Write the first two lines of a Christmas or winter poem. Have students brainstorm a list of words that rhyme with the last words in the lines. Then have them write one or two new lines to go with the first two. For example,

On the first day of Christmas

My true love gave to me

A crumpet and a steaming pot of tea.

          © *Teacher Created Materials, Inc. 1989*

Holiday Cornucopia

Materials: construction paper; scissors; white glue; glitter, lace, ribbon or other decorative items; stapler.

Directions:

- Cut a piece of construction paper using the pattern below.

- Form a cone shape and staple in two or three places.

- Drizzle glue on the outside of the cone; sprinkle glitter over the glue.

- Glue ribbon or lace or other decorative items onto the cone.

- Fill the cornucopia with popcorn or other treats.

- Optional: Hang the cornucopia from your Christmas tree. Punch a hole and thread yarn or ribbon through it.

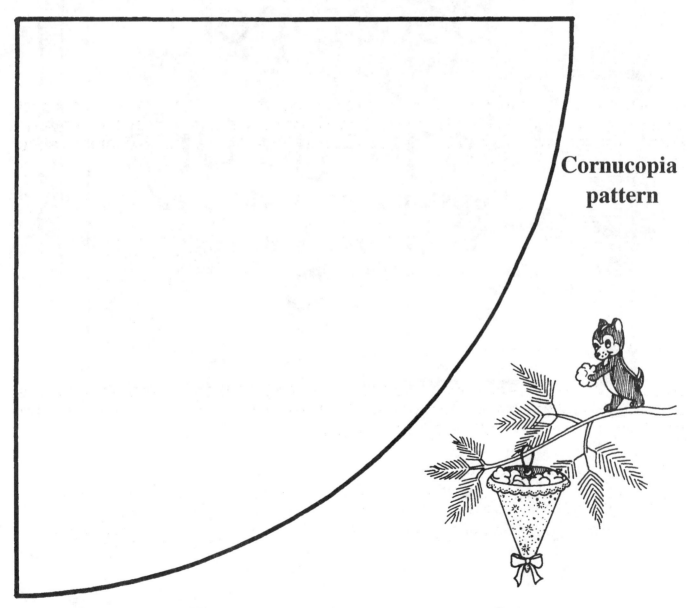

Cornucopia pattern

December Whole Language Unit

Christmas the World Over

- How to Write a Unit
- Lessons
- Worksheets
- And More!

Hot Tip!

Ask students to share the holiday customs of their native heritage. Have them bring in samples of holiday foods, native costumes, decorations, or songs and games, etc.

How to Plan

Christmas is a joyous occasion and a very special time of year. People the world over celebrate this holiday. Customs and traditions vary from country to country, but a festive spirit permeates the mood everywhere. Christmas presents a perfect opportunity for exploring other peoples, cultures, and beliefs. Begin your own Christmas unit by following these step-by-step guidelines.

 Set the mood in your classroom with an appropriate bulletin board. Pages 69 to 75 contain all the patterns you'll need to create a Christmas display (see diagram below).

 Assemble your resources: Books, films, tapes, games, texts, and real objects.

 Plan general lessons integrating math, reading, art, music, language, and physical education.

 Outline your lesson goals and objectives.

 Make evaluation tools that are appropriate for the lesson.

 After the first week of lessons, evaluate and then plan the next week.

Christmas the World Over

Projects and Lessons

The following pages describe specific lessons and ideas that can be used to integrate the curriculum through the study of Christmas.

- **Set up a display table** *with a decorated Christmas tree. Include ornaments from other countries or trim the tree with pictures of various customs. Also include some books on Christmas. Read related stories and poems aloud to the class.*

- **Keep parents informed** *about the class' upcoming activities. Compose a class letter to send home and have students copy the message on their own stationery (see diagram at right). Use the letter to enlist volunteers or request any necessary supplies you'll be needing throughout this unit.*

Language

- **Brainstorm with the students.** *Find out what they already know about Christmas. List all appropriate responses on the chalkboard or a flip chart. Use these ideas to plan specific lessons.*

Math

- **Display a clear plastic jar filled with lollipops,** *wrapped candy canes, or other treats. Have students estimate the number of candies in the jar. Make a class graph to record their responses. With older children, find out what fraction or percentage of students overestimated; find out what fraction or percentage of students underestimated. Count the candies; group them in tens on paper plates to reinforce place value.*

© *Teacher Created Materials, Inc. 1989*

Projects and Lessons

Language and Music

- **Sing some Christmas carols.** *Have students work in pairs or small groups. Each group chooses a song and writes out the words. Then they are to find and underline all nouns, replacing them with pronouns. Next, they must circle all adjectives and replace each with a synonym (or an antonym). Have each group share their re-written carol with the class — sing it!*

Social Studies

- **Research the following topics:** *Advent wreath, Christmas tree, Santa Claus, Santa Lucia Day, and Christmas caroling. Small groups or pairs can work together to find out the origins of these subjects, countries which observe these customs, and any special festivities that are celebrated. Have students draw pictures, make models, or bring in actual artifacts associated with their research topic.*

Art

- **Make stained-glass paper ornaments.** *Provide students with patterns from the Christmas Around the World Bulletin Board (pages 69 to 75). Direct them to place a piece of wax paper over one pattern. Cut one-inch squares of colored tissue paper. Dip a paint brush into liquid white glue and apply to a small area of the wax paper. Then glue a square at a time and fill in the whole shape. Make two or three layers of tissue for stability, overlap colors for an unusual effect. Allow to dry thoroughly. Lift the shape off of the wax paper. With scissors cut around the ornament to even up the jagged edges, if desired. Hang with thread or a metal Christmas ornament hanger.*

Creative Movement

- **Play some reindeer games.** *Have groups of students make up their own reindeer games or movements and teach them to the rest of the class.*

Projects and Lessons

Social Studies

- **Host an International Day!** *Group students to research the Christmas customs, foods, and symbols of a particular country. On a designated day, students display their projects and share them with the class or with other classrooms. Displays should include the country's flag, Christmas symbols, and some typical foods served. Students can dress in native costumes or show pictures of native dress. Original skits could be written to depict a special custom or celebration. Learn to say "Merry Christmas" in other languages! Take photographs or videotape the experience.*

Language

- **Use the Santa Claus creative writing shape** *(see page 55) for students to list gifts they would like to give to family members, world leaders, or famous people. Or have students write ways to make their own gifts. Or, have small groups make a list of all the smaller words they can make using the letters from the word ORNAMENT or HOLIDAY.*

Math and Science

- **Give each student a handful of colored Christmas candies.** *Separate all the red ones, all the green ones, etc. Which color do they have the most of? Which color do they have the least of? Have each student record his findings on a blank graph (see sample below). Make a composite class graph. Do word problems with the candies and tell students to count their candies as you say a problem. For example, "One elf had nine candies. Another elf had six. How many candies were there altogether?" (Students should make sets of nine and six candies and then put them together as you relate the story.)*

Color in or write the name of the color.

Color one space for each candy of the same color that is at the top of the column.

24

© Teacher Created Materials, Inc. 1989

Gingerbread Cookies

A playful elf mixed up the letters of some words in the cookie recipe below. See if you can fix the mess he made and write the correct word on the line next to each underlined word.

- *Cream ⅓ cup wrobn* _____ *sugar and ⅓ cup shortening until light and fluffy.*

- *Beat in ⅔ cup molasses and one unbeaten geg* _____ *.*

- *Sift in three cups loruf* _____ *, one tablespoon baking doepwr* _____ *, 1 ½ teaspoons ginger, and ½ teaspoon last* _____ *. Blend well.*

- *Chill for two shuro* _____ *.*

- *Divide gouhd* _____ *into fourths.*

- *Roll out to desired thinkness; cut with a ockoei* _____ *cutter.*

- *Place on a greased cookie these* _____ *and bake for five to seven stimune* _____ *at 350° F.*

- *Cool slightly before removing to a riwe* _____ *rack.*

- *Makes about two zoden* _____ *cookies.*

WORD BANK

egg	salt	flour
wire	brown	powder
cookie	sheet	minutes
dough	hours	dozen

Ask an adult at home to help you make these cookies!

Math Facts Review

front

back

Directions: Make as many gingerbread man shapes as you will need. Glue to heavy tagboard for durability; color and cut out. In the circle write an operation sign (see operation signs below) and the number you want to review (see diagram). Punch holes along the perimeter of the shape. Write a different number next to each hole punched. Turn the gingerbread man over and write the answers to the problems next to the proper hole. Laminate and cut out. Staple two craft sticks together to the bottom of each gingerbread man placing one stick on each side of the gingerbread man (see diagram).

To Play: One child faces the front of the gingerbread man, while another child faces the back of the gingerbread man shape. The child facing the front puts a pencil through a hole next to a number and says the problem aloud. (In the diagram, for example, each number will be divided by six. If the child puts the pencil in the 36, he would say, "Thirty-six divided by six equals six.") The child facing the back of the gingerbread shape checks the answers. After all problems have been computed, the children trade places.

Operation Signs: $+$, $-$, $\times$, $\div$

Name _____   Date _____

Gift Wrap

Santa's littlest elf has been busy wrapping Christmas presents. Write the answers to the questions below by reading the bar graph.

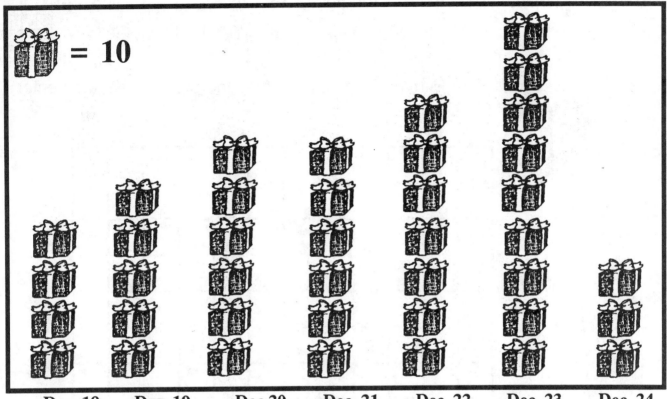

1. How many presents is one ![present] _____

2. How many presents were wrapped on December 24? _____

3. On which date were the most number of presents wrapped? _____

    How many presents is that altogether? _____

4. What is the difference between the number of presents wrapped

    on December 22 and on December 18? _____

5. How many total presents were wrapped on December

    18, 19, and 20? _____

6. On which dates were 60 presents wrapped each day? _____

CHALLENGE:

How many presents were wrapped altogether the whole week? _____

Name _____ **Date** _____

Winter Word Puzzle

Make your own crossword puzzle without clues. Connect all the words from the Word Bank so that they fit together like words in a crossword puzzle. Words may go across and down only. Adjacent lines may not touch. For example, is fine, but is not.

Hint: Start with the longest word first and place it near the center of the grid.

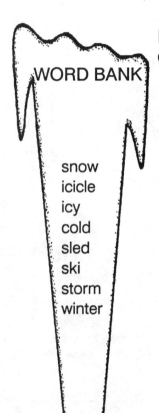

WORD BANK

snow
icicle
icy
cold
sled
ski
storm
winter

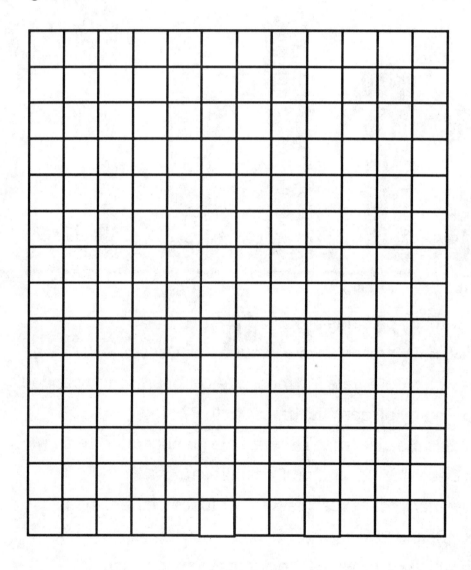

Choose a category such as Sports or Holidays. Make a list of ten related words and connect them. Use graph paper or draw your own grid.

© *Teacher Created Materials, Inc. 1989*

Name _____   **Skill** _____

Christmas Pictures

Write the name of each Christmas picture. Use the Word Bank to help you.

1.  _ _ _ _ _ _

2. _ _ _ _

3. _ _ _ _

4. _ _ _ _ _

5. _ _ _ _

6. _ _ _ _

7. _ _ _ _

8. 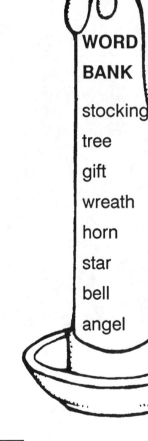 _ _ _ _ _ _ _ _

WORD BANK

stocking

tree

gift

wreath

horn

star

bell

angel

Challenge:

Write the plural of each word in the WORD BANK.

Name _____ Date _____

How to Write a Report

Use the steps outlined in this linear spiral to help you write a report.

WRITE FIVE QUESTIONS ABOUT THE TOPIC

1. On what day and month is it celebrated?
2. In which country is Boxing Day observed?
3. What is Boxing Day?
4. How did the custom originate?
5. How is it celebrated?

CHOOSE A TOPIC

Keep it specific. Holidays is too general; BOXING DAY is a specific holiday.

PUT THE QUESTIONS IN GOOD ORDER

3.
1.
2.
4.
5.

DO RESEARCH

Use a variety of books: Texts, biographies, encyclopedias, and other reference books. Write notes on index cards.

WRITE THE REPORT

Write four or five sentences about each of the five questions.

BIBLIOGRAPHY

At the end of your report write the title and author of all the books you researched.

YOUR TURN

- Choose a topic and write it on the line. _____

- Write five questions about the topic.

  1. _____
  2. _____
  3. _____
  4. _____
  5. _____

- Put the questions in good order.

1st _____ 2nd _____ 3rd _____ 4th _____ 5th _____

- Now you are ready to do research, write your report and bibliography.

© Teacher Created Materials, Inc. 1989

Creative Writing Pattern

Use this shape to record words that the class or small groups of students compile in brainstorming sessions. It can also be used for cooperative stories or individual writing.

December
People, Places, and Events

- ∘ **Christmas**
- ∘ **Boxing Day**
- ∘ **New Year's**
- ∘ **Hanukkah**
- ∘ **And more!**

The learning pages and ideas in this section are extensions of the people, places, and events from this month's calendar. They can be used to introduce a topic, reinforce or follow-up a lesson, or as independent projects. Many of these activities can easily be incorporated into your Whole Language program; others are suitable for cooperative learning projects.

Hot tips!

To make worksheets more challenging for your students, cover up the WORD BANK before duplicating the page.

If worksheets are too difficult for your students, add more clues before duplicating a page. Or, work together as a class. Write the words from the WORD BANK on the chalkboard. Have students go to the board and circle correct answers as the seated students write the correct answers on their worksheets.

Name _____   **Date** _____

December Greats

Write words or phrases from the WORD BANK that best tell about each December person below.

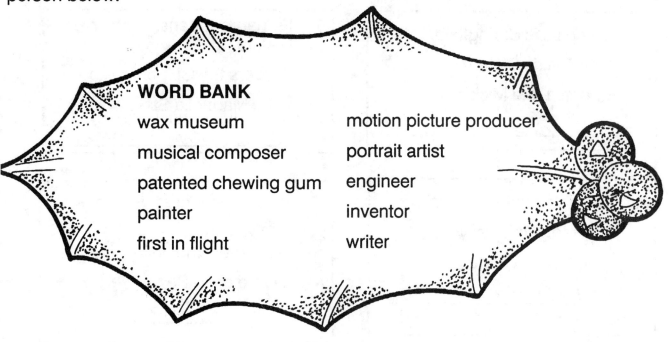

WORD BANK

wax museum	motion picture producer
musical composer	portrait artist
patented chewing gum	engineer
painter	inventor
first in flight	writer

1. Rudyard Kipling _____

2. Gilbert Stuart _____

3. William Semple _____

4. Madame Tussaud _____

5. Alexandre Gustave Eiffel _____

6. Ludwig van Beethoven _____

7. George Seurat _____

8. Wilbur and Orville Wright _____

9. Walt Disney _____

10. Eli Whitney _____

Teacher: This research page is an effective cooperative learning activity.

Name _____ **Date** _____

A Stately Month

Nine different states joined the United States during the month of December: Illinois, Delaware, Mississippi, Indiana, Pennsylvania, Alabama, New Jersey, Iowa, and Texas. Read the clues below and write the name of the correct state on the line.

1. Its capital is Springfield.

   "The Prairie State"

   Borders Lake Michigan

   _____

2. The state capital is Trenton.

   Princeton University

   "The Garden State"

   _____

3. Hoosiers

   Its name means "Land of the Indians."

   Home of the Indy 500

   _____

4. Named for Englishman William Penn

   Home of the Liberty Bell

   Is in the eastern part of U.S.

   _____

5. Its name means "Father of Waters."

   Borders the Gulf of Mexico

   "The Magnolia State"

   _____

6. The bluebonnet is the state flower.

   Its name is Indian for "friends."

   Home of NASA

   _____

7. The state capital is Montgomery.

   Home of Jefferson Davis

   Tuskegee Institute

   _____

8. "The Diamond State"

   Dover is its capital.

   The Ladybug is the state insect.

   _____

9. Des Moines is its capital. The state tree is the oak tree. "The Hawkeye State"

   _____

© Teacher Created Materials, Inc. 1989

Name _____ **Date** _____

The Eiffel Tower

(Birthdate of Alexandre Gustave Eiffel — December 15)

The Eiffel Tower was built in 1889 for the Paris International Exposition. It was designed by the French engineer Alexandre Gustav Eiffel. To find out what is at the top of this 1,000-foot-high tower, write the name of each picture in the spaces below it. Then use the numbers under the spaces as a code.

___ ___ ___ ___ ___
25 27 23   5 29

___ ___ ___ ___
13   5 19   7

___ ___ ___ ___
17 15 21 19

___ ___ ___
 9 11 11

The ___ ___ ___ ___ ___ ___ ___
        13 15 11 13   9 25 27

___ ___ ___   ___ ___ ___
13 21 27   7 21 11

in ___ ___ ___ ___ ___
      25 27   5 19   7

___ ___ ___   ___ ___ ___ ___ ___ !
27 13   9   29 21 23 17   7

Name _____ Date _____

Hanukkah

Hanukkah commemorates the victory of the Jewish people over the Syrians in the year 165 B.C. To celebrate, they lit the Temple lamp, which had barely enough oil for one day. Still, the lamp burned for eight days until more special oil could be prepared. Today, a special candleholder or menorah is used in an eight-day ceremony. Each day before sundown a candle is lit; each successive day, one more candle is lit.

The Festival of Lights, as Hanukkah is often called, is also a time for special dances, games, gifts, and food. A dreidel, or top, is a game enjoyed by children. Money, also know as gelt, is sometimes used in the game. (Gelt is chocolate wrapped in foil and packed in little net bags.) Latkes, or potato pancakes, are a tasty treat served with applesauce and sour cream.

Match the pictures in the center with their Hebrew words on the left and their common names on the right. Color the pictures.

latkes   candleholder

gelt   pancakes

dreidel   top

menorah   money

                          © *Teacher Created Materials, Inc. 1989*

You Can Draw It!

(Hanukkah)

Copy the picture one square at a time onto the bottom grid. Color your picture when you have finished your drawing.

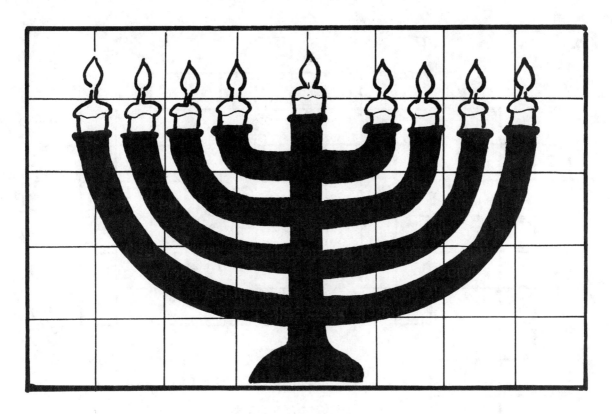

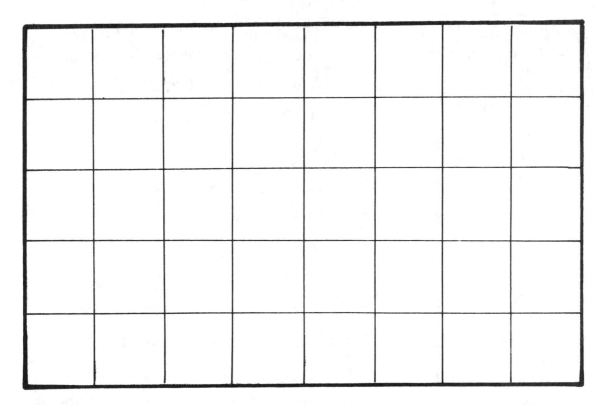

Name _____   Date _____

Holiday Crossword Puzzle

On December 21, 1913 the first crossword puzzle in an American newspaper appeared in the *New York Sunday World*. In honor of this historical event, solve the holiday crossword puzzle below. Some clues are given to help you.

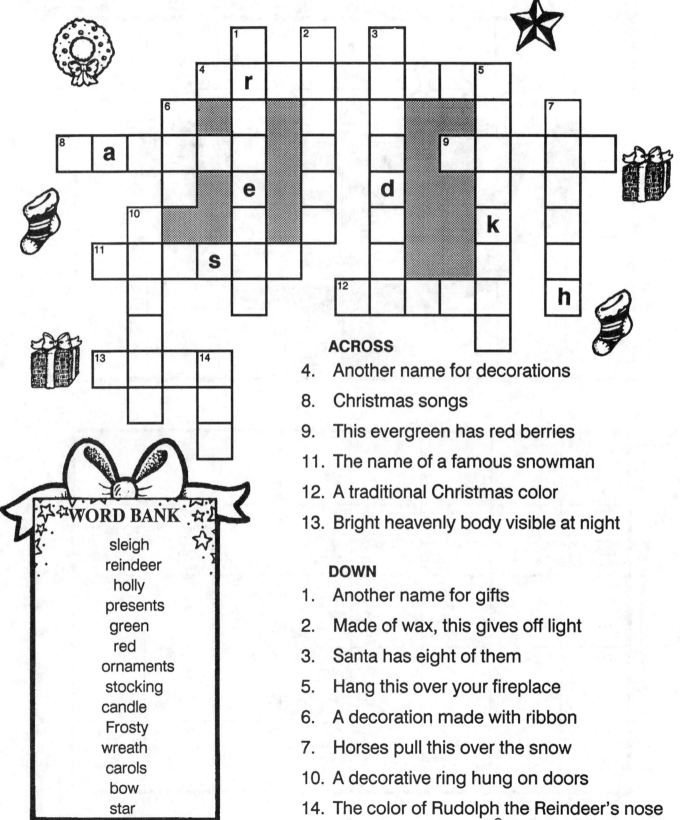

ACROSS

4. Another name for decorations
8. Christmas songs
9. This evergreen has red berries
11. The name of a famous snowman
12. A traditional Christmas color
13. Bright heavenly body visible at night

DOWN

1. Another name for gifts
2. Made of wax, this gives off light
3. Santa has eight of them
5. Hang this over your fireplace
6. A decoration made with ribbon
7. Horses pull this over the snow
10. A decorative ring hung on doors
14. The color of Rudolph the Reindeer's nose

WORD BANK

sleigh
reindeer
holly
presents
green
red
ornaments
stocking
candle
Frosty
wreath
carols
bow
star

© *Teacher Created Materials, Inc. 1989*

Think Snow!

(Dec. 21, First Day of Winter)

Each group of letters below has something to do with snow. Make words out of each group by filling in the blanks with only those letters on the handle. Use each letter only once and cross it off when you use it.

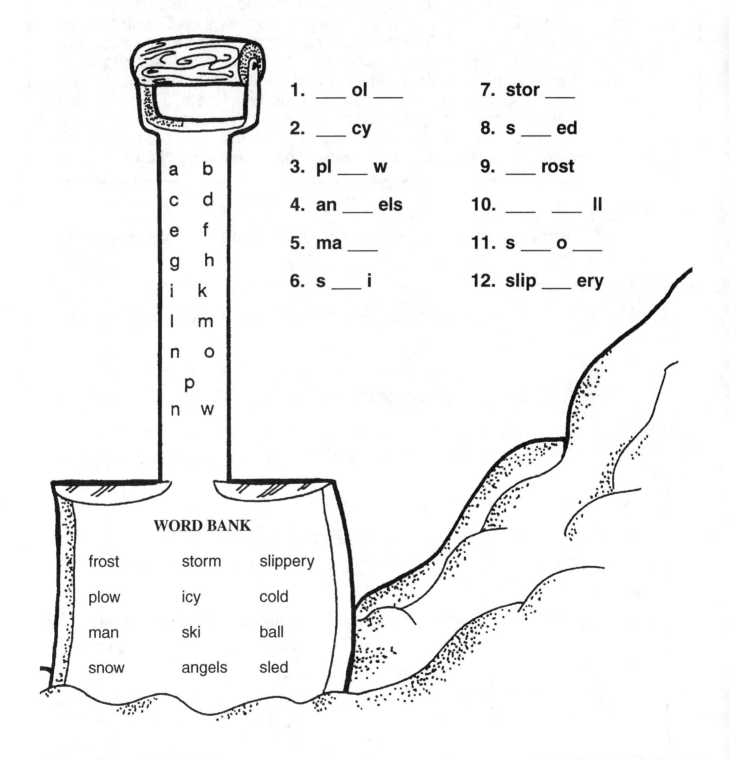

1. ___ ol ___

2. ___ cy

3. pl ___ w

4. an ___ els

5. ma ___

6. s ___ i

7. stor ___

8. s ___ ed

9. ___ rost

10. ___ ___ ll

11. s ___ o ___

12. slip ___ ery

Letters on handle:
a b
c d
e f
g h
i k
l m
n o
p
n w

WORD BANK

frost	storm	slippery
plow	icy	cold
man	ski	ball
snow	angels	sled

Name _____ **Date** _____

Christmas Customs Around the World

Many of the Christmas traditions that we observe today actually began in other countries years ago. They were brought to the United States and Canada by the immigrants who settled there.

The Christmas tree, for example, began in Germany in 1605 and was the idea of Martin Luther. His tree was simply decorated with lighted candles. Cornucopias are an English tradition. They stand for the happiness of giving to others at Christmas time. The custom of hanging stockings on Christmas Eve comes to us from Greece. A Greek legend says that St. Nicholas, a bishop, dropped gold down a man's chimney where it landed in his oldest daughter's stocking. In France, gonfalons or brightly colored banners greet visitors. These banners are usually hung on doors and proclaim "Joyeux Noël". The poinsettia came to the United States from Mexico. Dr. Joel Poinsett brought one to South Carolina in 1828 and it quickly became a holiday favorite. In Spain, bells are rung to announce Christmas Eve and homes are decorated with a Nativity scene.

1. **Knowledge**

    Name a Christmas custom from each country: England, France, Mexico, Spain, and Germany.

2. **Comprehension**

    Explain how so many different customs came to be observed in the United States and Canada.

3. **Application**

    Make a gonfalon or draw a picture of one.

4. **Analysis**

    Compare and contrast two Christmas customs. How are they alike? How are they different?

5. **Synthesis**

    Create a poster that shows a map of different countries of the world and the Christmas custom that originated there.

6. **Evaluation**

    Write a paragraph explaining which Christmas custom is your favorite and why.

Amazing Stocking

Find your way through the stocking maze. Color the toys and gifts when you are through.

Hot Tip!

Make an art project with this pattern. Color and glue to tagboard; cut out. Punch evenly spaced holes around the outside of the stocking. Thread red yarn in and out of the holes for a decorative effect.

Hidden Answers

(Christmas, December 25)

Using only the letters from the word in the middle picture, name the eight other pictures.

Decorations

Name _____   Date _____

Wrap It!

Find and circle the gift in each row that is just the right size to fit into the package at the beginning of the row. Color all the gifts that you think children would enjoy.

Boxing Day

(The first weekday after Christmas)

Boxing Day is a holiday celebrated on the first weekday after Christmas. Special boxed gifts are given to household and public servants. This holiday is observed in Canada, Australia, and New Zealand.

To find out where Boxing Day was first celebrated, follow the directions below.

Write the name of each picture in the squares that go DOWN from that picture.

Then fill in the blank squares ACROSS.

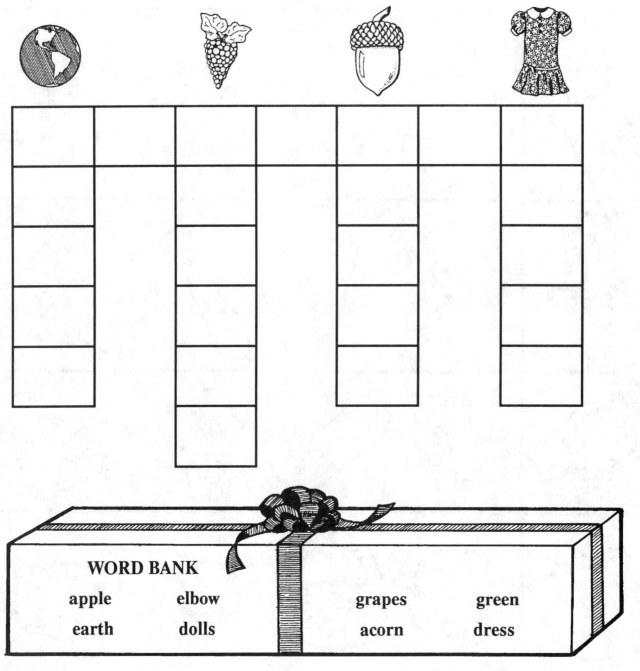

WORD BANK

apple	elbow	grapes	green
earth	dolls	acorn	dress

Name _____   Date _____

New Year's Eve Dot - to - Dot

(December 31)

Connect the dots. Color the picture.

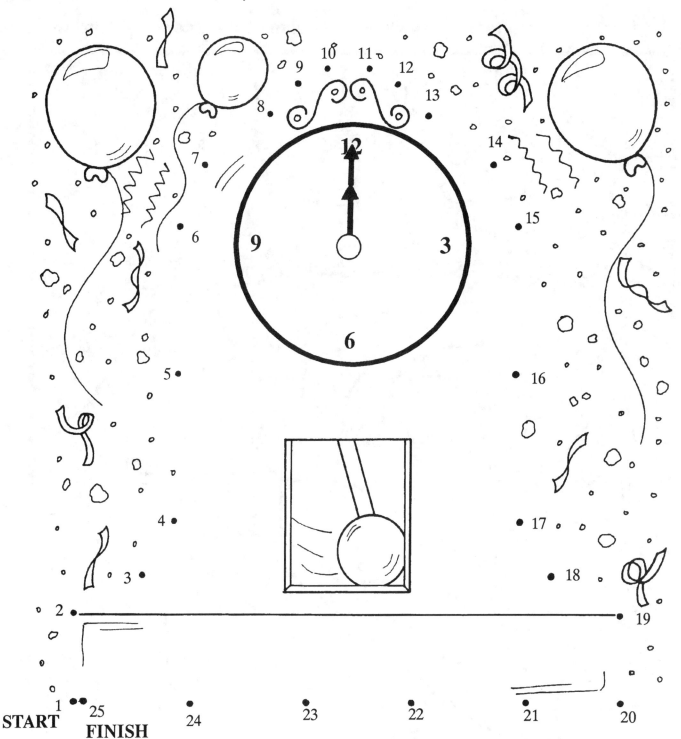

Holiday Scene

Color the numbers the correct color and a holiday scene will appear!

1 - red   2 - orange   3 - yellow   4 - blue   5 - green   6 - brown

December Management

- Clip Art
- Contracts and Awards
- Holiday Report Form
- A Month of Writing
- And More!

Hot Tip!

Promote good will among your students. Plan a class project to do something nice for another group. For example, have a Food Drive for some needy families in the area. Or plan an afternoon of Christmas caroling at a Senior Citizen's Center. Or bring in used but still-in-good-condition toys to be distributed to needy youngsters.

Name _____   Date _____

A Month of Writing

Spark students' imaginations with this month's list! Each day write a different title on the board and with the class brainstorm words that could be associated with that title. Record the words on a chart for easy reference. Instruct students to write a poem or creative story using the day's title and words from the class' list. For maximum enjoyment, make this a cooperative learning activity and group students to work together. Award prizes for the longest story, the funniest story, the most sensible story, etc.

1	Deck the Halls	16.	All I Want for Christmas
2.	I'm Dreaming of a White Christmas	17.	Winter Wonderland
3.	Sleigh Ride	18.	Rudolph the Red-Nose Reindeer
4.	I'll Be Home for Christmas	19.	Silver Bells
5.	Jingle Bell Rock	20.	Up on a Roof Top
6.	The First Noel	21.	Feliz Navidad
7.	O Little Town of Bethlehem	22.	Frosty the Snow Man
8.	Blue Christmas	23.	Greensleeves
9.	O Christmas Tree	24.	Silent Night
10.	Jolly Old St. Nicholas	25.	Away in a Manger
11.	Santa Claus Is Coming to Town	26.	We Three Kings of Orient Are
12.	Hark, the Herald Angels Sing	27.	Let It Snow
13.	Do They Know It's Christmas?	28.	Jingle Bells
14.	God Rest Ye Merry Gentlemen	29.	I Saw Mommy Kissing Santa Claus
15.	The Twelve Days of Christmas	30.	Good King Wenceslaus

Name_____ **Date**_____

Favorite Book Report

Choose your favorite character from a book you have just read. Then, based on what you've read, write what you think some of your character's favorite things might be.

Character's name _____

Brief description _____

_____

These are a few of _____'s favorite things.

(Character's name)

favorite food: _____

favorite toy: _____

favorite game to play: _____

favorite place to go: _____

favorite song to sing: _____

favorite friend: _____

favorite subject: _____

favorite color: _____

favorite music: _____

favorite hobby: _____

favorite sport: _____

favorite animal: _____

A Growing Experiment

Children will enjoy this cooperative holiday science lesson. Allow at least three weeks for seeds to grow.

Materials

- one pine cone for each group of students
- potting soil
- grass seeds
- large container of water
- foam cups
- trays (pie plates, foam meat trays, etc.)
- spray bottle with water

Directions:

1. Group students into small groups of three or four.

2. Have one student from each group hold their pine cone under water to allow pine cone to open up.

3. With foam cups, measure one cupful of soil and one half cupful of grass seed.

4. Take the pine cone out of the water and stand it up in its tray; fill the tray with water.

5. Sprinkle the pine cone evenly with the soil; then sprinkle the grass seed over that.

6. Label the outside of tray with group members' names (write on masking tape).

7. The students will need to check on their pinecones daily to make sure that there is water in the pan. They will also need to mist their pine cones.

8. Every other day have students record changes in the seeds and in the growth of the grass. Depending on their level, students can draw pictures, write about the changes, and actually measure growth and record it on a graph.

 The Science Experiment Form (page 51) can also be used with this activity.

Science Experiment Form

Name(s) _____

Title of Experiment _____

Question

?

What do we want to find out?

_____
_____
_____

Hypothesis

What do we think we will find out?

_____
_____
_____
_____

Procedure

How will we find out? (List step by step)

1. _____
   _____

2. _____
   _____

3. _____
   _____
   _____

4. _____
   _____
   _____

Results

What actually happened?

_____
_____
_____
_____

Conclusions   What did we learn? _____

_____
_____
_____

Name _____ **Date** _____

Holiday Report

Name of holiday _____

Date it is celebrated _____

Date it was first celebrated _____

Historical events and people that led to its celebration

_____

_____

Type of holiday (circle answers):   local   state   national   religious

Draw some symbols of this holiday.	**List any stories, poems, or songs associated with this holiday.** _____ _____ _____ _____ _____ _____ _____ _____
This holiday's colors and what they mean. _____ _____ _____ _____ _____ _____ _____	**Traditions, customs, or celebrations associated with this holiday.** _____ _____ _____ _____ _____ _____ _____

© *Teacher Created Materials, Inc. 1989*

Angel

This cheerful Christmas angel makes a delightful decoration for home or classroom!

Directions:

1. Color

2. Cut out.

3. Paste X's together as shown in diagram.

4. Decorate with glitter.

Finger Puppets

Directions:

1. Reproduce on white construction paper.

2. Color and cut out.

3. Cut along dashed lines.

4. Fasten finger puppet around finger with tape.

© *Teacher Created Materials, Inc. 1989*

Santa Creative Writing Pattern

Attach the lined "beard" on page 56 to Santa's face. Have children write holiday poems, stories, or letters to Santa!

Santa Creative Writing

December Record form

NAME													

December Bookmarks

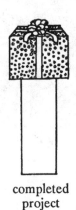

completed
project

Materials:

- bookmark pattern
- tagboard
- crayons or colored markers
- scissors

Directions:

Note: Make a pattern out of tagboard. Have the child use this pattern to make his own bookmark.

1. Trace around pattern onto tagboard.

2. Draw an object, animal, or other shape in the square at the top of the bookmark pattern. (Supply the three patterns on this page, if desired.)

3. Cut out.

4. Color the design with crayons or marking pens.

bookmark
pattern

Have students record the names of some of their favorite characters from books they have read onto the handle of the Book mark.

58 © Teacher Created Materials, Inc. 1989

Holiday Gift Tags

Color and cut out. Punch out holes. Thread with yarn or ribbon and attach to a gift.

Homework!

Write your assignments in the spaces below. Check them off as you complete them.

Reading

Mon. _____

Tues. _____

Wed. _____

Thurs. _____

Fri. _____

Language

Mon. _____

Tues. _____

Wed. _____

Thurs. _____

Fri. _____

Math

Mon. _____

Tues. _____

Wed. _____

Thurs. _____

Fri. _____

Science

Mon. _____

Tues. _____

Wed. _____

Thurs. _____

Fri. _____

Social Studies

Mon. _____

Tues. _____

Wed. _____

Thurs. _____

Fri. _____

Other

Mon. _____

Tues. _____

Wed. _____

Thurs. _____

Fri. _____

© Teacher Created Materials, Inc. 1989

You're Invited

Thank You

Contract / Award

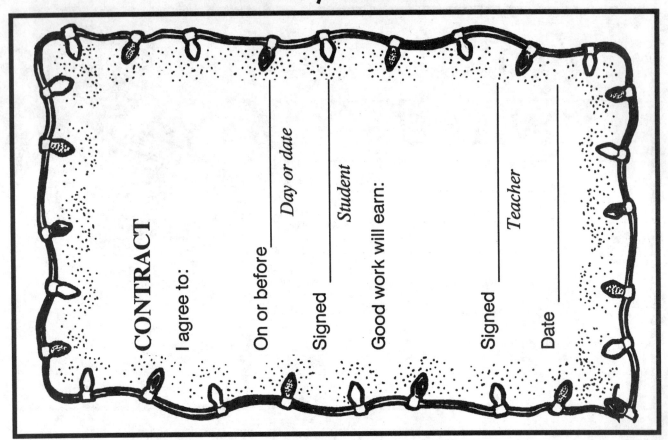

CONTRACT

I agree to:

On or before _____
                     Day or date

Signed _____
                Student

Good work will earn:

Signed _____
                Teacher

Date _____

AWARD

This is to certify that _____

                                    Name

did EXCELLENT WORK in:

Congratulations!

_____

Teacher

© *Teacher Created Materials, Inc. 1989*

We're Going On A Field Trip!

Where: _____

_____

When: _____

_____

Why: _____

_____

How: _____

_____

Please bring: _____

_____

_____

Please sign the permission slip below and have your child return it by _____. Your child will not be allowed to go without this slip.

Thank you.

_____
Teacher

✂ -

My child, _____, has my permission to participate in the field trip to _____.

_____
Parent

☐ I would like to chaperone. Please contact me!

DECEMBER NEWS!

© Teacher Created Materials, Inc. 1989

Big Patterns

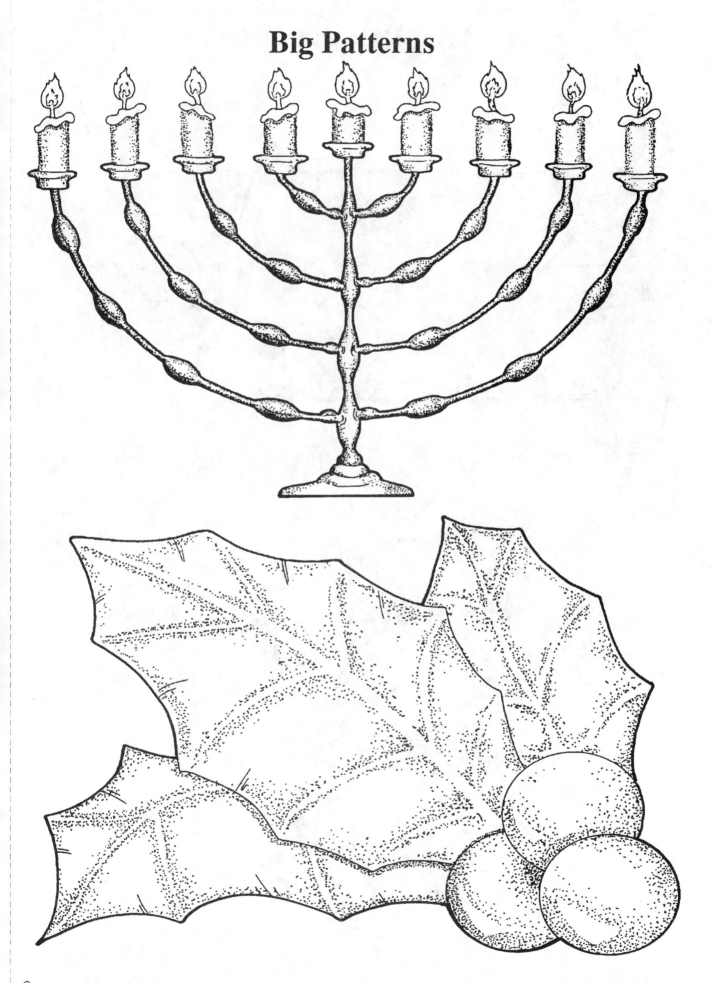

Big Patterns

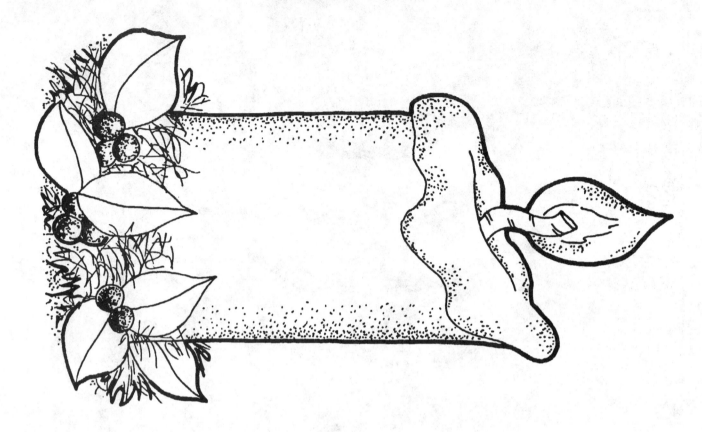

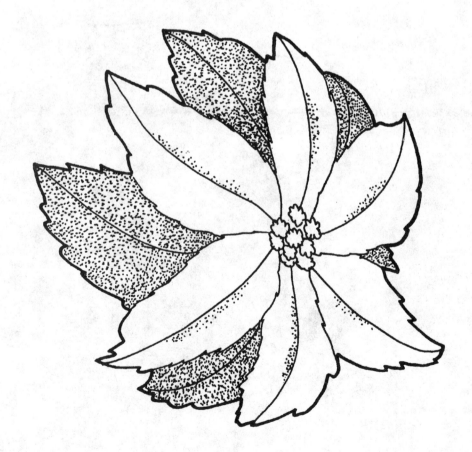

66

© Teacher Created Materials, Inc. 1989

Big Patterns

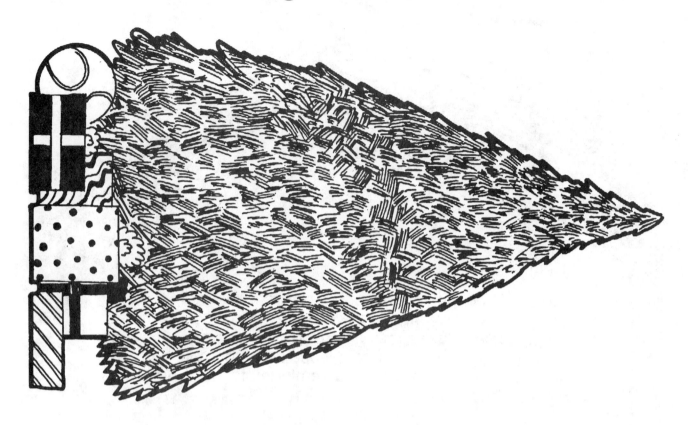

© Teacher Created Materials, Inc. 1989

Dear Parents,

Our class will be making lots of fun projects this month. Many of our activities will require items you may already have at home. Would you please take a minute and see if you have any of the following items on hand? If so, please send them in with your child. Then keep this list as a reminder to help our class throughout the month.

_____

Teacher

Thank You!

December
Bulletin Board

- Complete Directions
- Patterns
- Suggested Uses

 Hot Tip!

Combine math and art with this cooperative learning project: Make a paper chain that has one thousand links (or any other number you choose). Have students predict how far it will reach (use standerd or metric measure) and how long it will take them to make a chain that length.

OBJECTIVES

This interactive bulletin board can be used to teach or reinforce facts about other countries and their Christmas customs. Some suggestions are given below.

Materials

- *thick, green craft yarn*
- *stapler*
- *scissors*
- *Optional: Popcorn or cranberry garland*

Construction

- *Duplicate patterns and glue to tagboard. Color and cut out.*
- *Make a Christmas tree outline with the yarn; staple to background.*
- *Attach ornaments to the tree.*
- *Draw or make yarn garlands.*

Directions

- *Assign a different ornament to each group of students. Have them label their ornament on the bulletin board with the name of the country; have them write a short report on the origin of that custom.*

Hot Tips!

Students can thread popped popcorn or fresh cranberries (or both for a truly festive look!) to make a decorative garland for the tree.

Students can make additional ornaments using construction paper, glitter, and felt pens.

     © *Teacher Created Materials, Inc. 1989*

Christmas the World Over

(cont.)

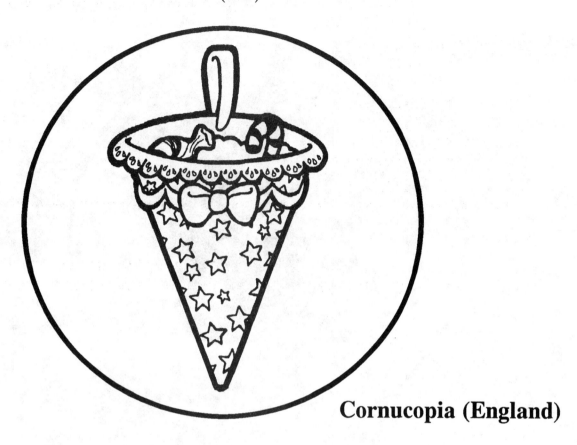

Cornucopia (England)

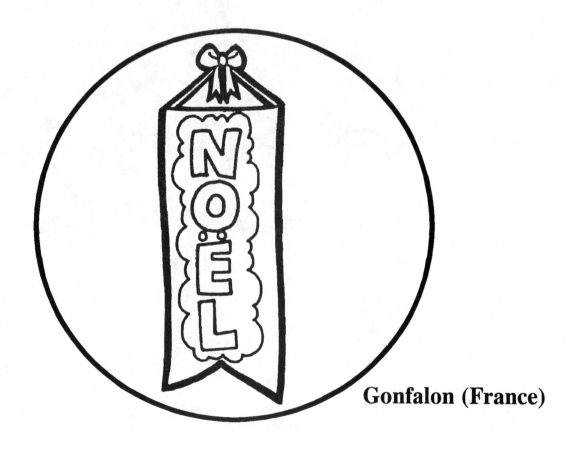

Gonfalon (France)

Christmas the World Over

(cont.)

Christmas tree (Germany)

Angel (Czechoslovakia)

© *Teacher Created Materials, Inc. 1989*

Christmas the World Over

(cont.)

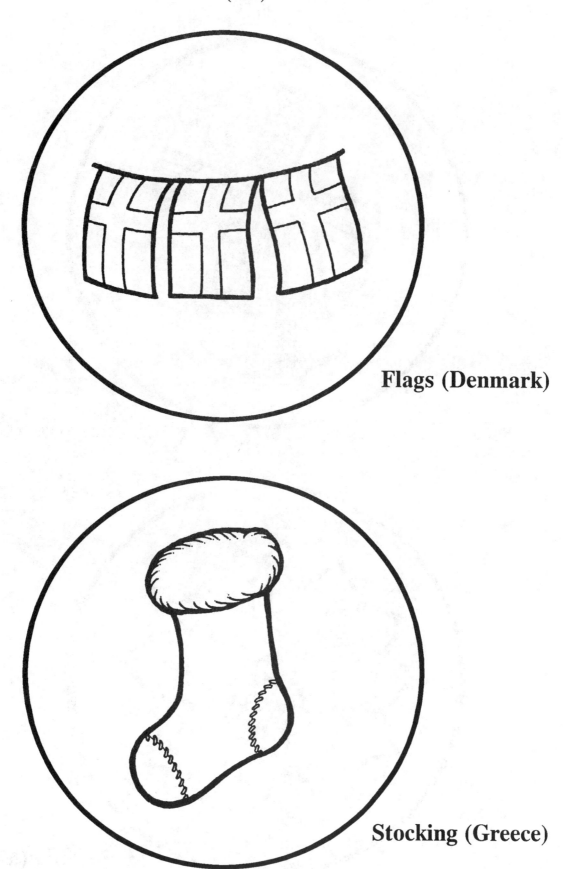

Flags (Denmark)

Stocking (Greece)

Christmas the World Over

(cont.)

Windmill (Holland)

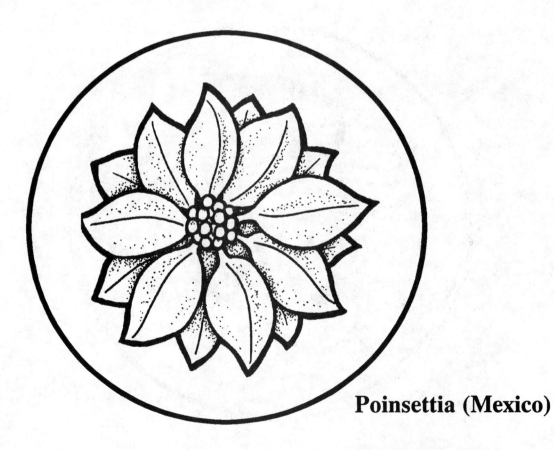

Poinsettia (Mexico)

Christmas the World Over

(cont.)

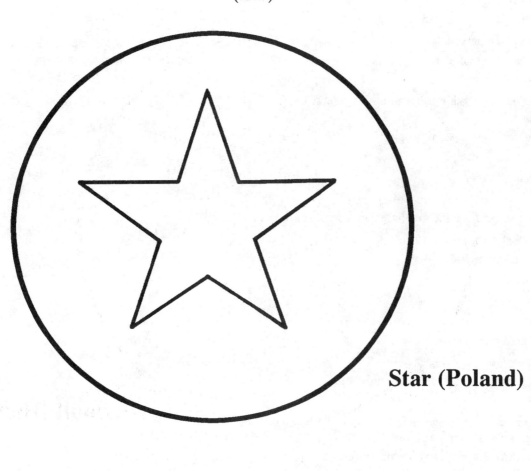

Star (Poland)

Bluebird (Sweden)

December Answer Key to Calendar Events

1. Answers will vary.
2. Using dots of color instead of brushstrokes
3. A likeness of a person, usually just the head
4. Labor Day (September)
5. Orlando, FL
6. A fourth-century bishop known for his kindness to children
7. Wax figures of prominent people
8. Mass production
9. Answers will vary.
10. Jackson
11. A word formed from the first letters of several words
12. Central America
13. Norway, Sweden, Italy
14. Antarctica
15. 1,000 ft.
16. Hearing
17. Less than one minute
18. Slavery
19. Decimal, decimeter, decade, decennial, etc.
20. France
21. A word made by rearranging letters within a word. For example, an anagram for pest is step or pets.
22. People who could not pay their debts were sent to colonize Georgia.
23. 192 hours; 11,520 minutes
24. Franz Gruber
25. Answers will vary.
26. Answers will vary.
27. Pasteurization
28. Answers will vary.
29. Lone Star State
30. A boy raised by jungle animals.
31. Answers will vary.

p. 15

1. candy cane
2. gingerbread
3. reindeer
4. snowflake
5. wreath
6. elf
7. holly
8. gifts
9. carols
10. star

p. 25

brown, egg, flour, powder, salt, hours, dough, cookie, sheet, minutes, wire, dozen

P. 27

1. 10
2. 30
3. Dec. 23; 90
4. 30
5. 150
6. Dec. 20 & 21

CHALLENGE: 400

p. 29

1. wreath
2. bell
3. star
4. angel
5. tree
6. gift
7. horn
8. stocking

p. 33

1. writer
2. portrait artist
3. patented chewing gum
4. wax museum
5. engineer
6. musical composer
7. painter
8. first in flight
9. motion picture producer
10. inventor

p. 34

1. Illinois
2. New Jersey
3. Indiana
4. Pennsylvania
5. Mississippi
6. Texas

7. Alabama
8. Delaware
9. Iowa

p. 35 straw, hand, lion, egg — The highest hot dog stand in the world!

p. 36

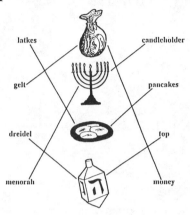

latkes
candleholder
gelt
pancakes
dreidel
top
menorah
money

P. 38

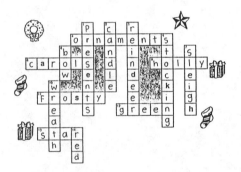

p. 39

1. cold
2. icy
3. plow
4. angels
5. man
6. ski
7. storm
8. sled
9. frost
10. ball
11. shoe
12. slippery

p. 42

1. car
2. nest
3. star
4. door
5. corn
6. train
7. deer
8. notes

p. 43

The computer, kite, baseball bat, sled, and beach ball should be circled.

p. 44

E	n	g	l	a	n	d
a		r		c		r
r		a		o		e
t		p		r		s
h		e		n		s
		s				

Open Worksheets Skills

These pages are ready to use. Simply fill in the directions and write the skill you want to reinforce. Make a copy for each student or pair of students or glue the worksheet to tagboard and laminate. Place at an appropriate classroom center; students can use water-based pens for easy wipe off and subsequent use. Ideas and resources for programming these worksheets are provided below and on the following pages.

Math

Basic facts
Comparing numbers and fractions
Decimals
Word Problems
Time
Place Value
Skip counting
Ordinal numbers (1st, 2nd, 3rd, etc.)

Sets
Missing addends
Money Problems
Geometric shapes
Measurement
Word names for numbers
Sequence
Percent

Roman Numerals

I - 1
II - 2
III - 3
IV - 4
V - 5

VI - 6
VII - 7
VIII - 8
IX - 9
X - 10

L - 50
C - 100
D - 500
M - 1,000
$\overline{\text{L}}$ - 50,000

Metric Measurement

mm - millimeter (1/10 cm)
cm - centimeter (10 mm)
dm - decimeter (10 cm)
m - meter (1,000 mm)
km - kilometer (1,000 m)

g - gram
kg - kilogram (1,000 g)
L-liter (1,000 mL)
mL - milliliter
cc - cubic centimeter

Measurement Equivalents

12 in. = 1 ft.
3 ft. = 1 yd.
5,280 ft. = 1 mi.

4 qt. = 1 gal.
2 pt. = 1 qt.
8 oz. = 1 c.

1 t. = 2,000 lbs.
60 sec. = 1 min.
60 min. - 1 hr.

© Teacher Created Materials, Inc. 1989

Open Worksheet Skills

(cont.)

Abbreviations

Names of states	dr. - drive	mt. - mountain
Days of the week	ave. - avenue	p. - page
Units of measurement	Dr. - Doctor	etc. - et cetera
Months of the year	Mrs. - Misses	yr. - year
blvd. - boulevard	Mr. - Mister	wk. - week
rd. - road	Gov. - Governor	
st. - street	Pres. - President	

Contractions

isn't - is not	I've - I have	they'd - they would
doesn't - does not	we've - we have	you'll - you will
haven't - have not	I'm - I am	won't - will not
hasn't - has not	you're - you are	I'm - I am
that's - that is	it's - it is	let's - let us

Compound Words

airplane	bodyguard	everywhere	percent
anyhow	bookcase	footnote	quarterback
anything	cardboard	grandfather	snowflake
basketball	classroom	handwriting	suitcase
bedroom	earthquake	makeup	watermelon

Prefixes

dis -	un -	over -	re -
disapprove	uncut	overcharge	recover
discolor	uneven	overdressed	redo
discount	unfair	overdue	reheat
dislike	unhappy	overfeed	remiss
dismay	unlike	overgrown	replay
dismiss	unmade	overpaid	reset
disobey	unwashed	overrun	review

Suffixes

- ful	- less	- ly	- en
beautiful	ageless	actively	harden
careful	homeless	happily	moisten
helpful	priceless	quickly	sweeten
skillful	worthless	silently	thicken

© Teacher Created Materials, Inc. 1989

Open Worksheet Skills

(cont.)

Plurals

- s

toe	kitten
pin	window
lamp	star
book	key

- es

church	class
lunch	inch
box	tomato
brush	waltz

- ies

sky	cherry
baby	body
party	army
family	lady

Anagrams

dear - dare - read
notes - stone - tones
fowl - flow - wolf
veil - vile - evil - live
tea - ate - eat

shoe - hoes - hose
vase - save
pea - ape
north - thorn
flea - leaf

veto - vote
cone - once
stop - tops - pots - post - spot
steam - meats - mates - tames

Synonyms

sleepy - tired
firm - solid
story - tale
shut - close
easy - simple

wealthy - rich
quick - fast
sea - ocean
icy - cold
chore - task

friend - pal
tiny - small
jump - leap
gift - present
hike - walk

Antonyms

empty - full
tame - wild
city - country
faster - slower
strong - weak

tall - short
rough - smooth
light - dark
dirty - clean
calm - nervous

correct - wrong
forget - remember
thick - slender
sweet - sour
young - aged

Homonyms

eight - ate
whole - hole
red - read
hour - our
peace - piece

lone - loan
pale - pail
knew - new
nose - knows
blew - blue

would - wood
for - four - fore
by - buy - bye
sense - cents - scents
two - too - to

80

© Teacher Created Materials, Inc. 1989